Wonderworker

The True Story of How Saint Nicholas Became Santa Claus

Vincent A. Yzermans

ACTA

ASSISTING CHRISTIANS TO ACT

PUBLICATIONS

Wonderworker
The True Story of How Saint Nicholas Became Santa Claus
by Msgr. Vincent A. Yzermans

Cover design by Tom A. Wright
Interior design by Br. Placid Stuckenschneider, O.S.B.
Typesetting by Robert Briggs
Printing by Park Press Quality Printing, Inc.

ACTA Publications
Assisting Christians To Act
4848 N. Clark Street
Chicago, IL 60640
800-397-2282
actapublications@aol.com
www.actapublications.com

ISBN: 0-87946-278-7
Library of Congress number 2004110462
Printed in the United States of America.
Year: 10 09 08 07 06 05 04
Printing: 10 9 8 7 6 5 4 3 2 1

TABLE OF CONTENTS

FOREWORD

January 2, 1994

My Dear Great-Nephew Nicholas,

LAST CHRISTMAS I HAD DINNER WITH YOU AND YOUR FAMILY AT the home of your grandparents. After dinner we opened gifts and you received a toy spaceship. You played with it under the Christmas tree, guiding it through an imaginary outer space.

I called you over to my chair and asked who gave you the spaceship.

"Santa Claus," you replied.

"Do you know who St. Nicholas is?" I asked.

"Nope."

Your grandmother said, "For gosh sakes, he's only three years old!"

You then returned to your spaceship and the conversation among adults continued. After some time I called you over to my chair again. You came twirling the spaceship above your head.

"Nicholas, I am going to write you a Christmas book next year. It will be about St. Nicholas and Santa Claus." I knew you did not understand what I was saying but you did inspire me to undertake this book.

Your grandmother interjected, "He can't read."

"That's all right," I replied. "He will when he's thirteen or fourteen. Writers create for the ages, not the years." A touch of grandiosity there!

So, Nicholas, this book is for you.

Your loving great-uncle:

Vincent A. Yzermans

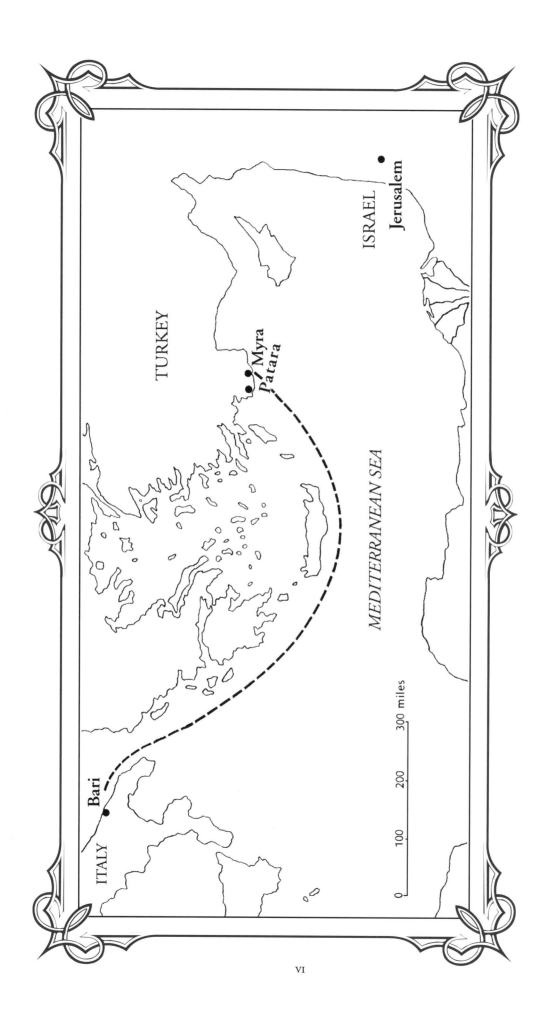

NICHOLAS THE YOUTH

MANY GOOD STORIES BEGIN WITH "ONCE UPON A time." This is a good story because it tells the life and travels of a remarkable man whom almost everyone knows. His story – which is also our story – begins, as Dickens wrote in *A Tale of Two Cities*, neither in the best of times nor in the worst of times. The times then were very much like our times now. The year was 280 A.D.

In that year the western known world was centered around that body of water which the ancients called the "Sea in the Middle of the World." Today we call it the Mediterranean Sea. At the time we are describing we called this area the Roman Empire, including its borderlands Asia Minor, northern Africa, Europe and distant Britannia.

The empire was pagan, at least officially, worshipping false gods, sometimes at the command of the emperors. Those who refused were imprisoned, exiled, beheaded or crucified. Nero burned *the* City – Rome – in 67 A.D. He blamed the conflagration on the members of the new sect called Christians who were proscribed and persecuted. This created for the early Christian Church the Age of Martyrs which continued for more than two hundred years.

In the year 280 Christians were being imprisoned and martyred during the last, and perhaps the most violent, persecution, under Emperor Diocletian who resigned in 305. He demanded that Christians worship him as a god, the son of Jupiter. In 303 he ordered that Christian churches and all their sacred books be burned and that Christian believers be either imprisoned, enslaved or executed.

The emperor was a dictator; his will and commands were absolute, reaching down to the smallest village, affecting countless, nameless people. He ruled through governors he appointed as his representatives in various provinces of the empire. One of these provinces was called Lycia which touched the eastern shore of the Sea in the Middle of the World. Its capital was a thriving city called Myra and its adjacent seaport was called Andeiki. Today there is no seaport and Myra has changed its name to Demre. This is the locale of the first part of this story.

Myra is located in modern Turkey at the foot of the 10,000 foot peaks of the Taurus Mountains which drop abruptly into the sea. The coastland is rugged, making safe harbors rare. The area was a graveyard for many ships which sailed the coastal route, carrying grain to Constantinople and Rome from the wheatfields of Egypt. It was also one of the centers of worship of Artemis, the Greek goddess of fertility.

Tradition tells us that St. Paul the Apostle visited Patara, one of seaports established by the Greeks as a necklace around Myra. The emperor was unknowingly assisting Paul's apostolate by shedding the blood of human martyrs. For this reason Origen, an early Christian writer, wrote: "The blood of martyrs becomes the seed of Christians." The more the emperor unsheathed his sword, the more pagan people found their way to the living waters of baptism throughout the empire.

Nonna and Epiphanius were a couple numbered among the Christians in Patara. An ancient writer described them as "devoted Christians, not so poor as to be scorned by others, but neither so rich as to be boastful; they had enough to support themselves and still give to the poor." They were descendants of the original colony of Christians established by St. Paul. They spent thirty years praying that they might be blessed with a child. Their prayers were answered in 280 by the birth of a son, their only child.

They named him Nicholas in honor of his priest-uncle who was the superior of a monastery in Xanthos, a neighboring village. Already in the third century the name Nicholas was common among the early Christians. It was rooted in the origins of the Christian Church, for a man by that name being chosen as one of the first deacons.

As a boy Nicholas frequently visited his uncle, assisting in chanting prayers and participating in religious services. The child advanced in secular learning from the local school and acquired religious knowledge through the instructions of his parents and the monks at his uncle's monastery. His parents, however, died when Nicholas was still a youth and left him a substantial inheritance. Nicholas the priest assumed the care of his young nephew. He brought the young man to live with him in the monastery. After a few more years, Nicholas asked to be admitted as a monk into the religious community. His uncle told him that he must dispose of his wealth before being admitted into the brotherhood.

This admonition caused two events in the young Nicholas' life which, in time, become the foundation of his future reputation. The first involved three maidens in his native village; the other, aboard ship along the trade routes of the Sea in the Middle of the World.

News, especially bad news, travels fast. Nicholas heard about the great misfortune that had stricken one of his neighbors and his three daughters. The neighbor, once a wealthy man, had been reduced to a state of dire poverty. Without any finances he lacked the necessary money to provide dowries for his three marriageable daughters. He could see nothing in their future except selling them into slavery or forcing them to support themselves as prostitutes. The prospect of these options drove him into a state of despair and his daughters into a condition of constant distress.

Still a very young man, with his parents' inheritance in reserve, Nicholas determined to assist his neighbor in his seemingly hopeless dilemma. He filled three small bags with gold coins. In the early hours of the morning when the entire village was asleep, he passed by the window of the bedroom in which the three maidens slept. He tossed one bag filled with gold into the window.

Rapture filled the distressed man's house the next morning. The happiness of the man and his daughters made Nicholas extremely happy. The next night he repeated the same action. Again the father's house was flooded with joy. By this time the elated man resolved to discover who their munificent benefactor might be. He waited and watched during the third night.

He saw the youth throw a third bag of gold in the window. At the same time Nicholas discovered the man lurking in the shadows. Nicholas ran as fast as he could, so as not to be discovered. The father ran even faster and caught up with the youth.

"Please," Nicholas pleaded, "do not tell anyone of this deed as long as I live. I hold you responsible in the presence of God, to keep my secret safe."

We do not know whether or not the maidens' father kept the secret until after Nicholas' death. We do know, however, that this is one of the earliest recorded events in the young man's life. It had nothing to do with the miraculous, as the following story has, but was a simple and generous act of gift-giving. By such acts of charity Nicholas, in time, would become the greatest gift-giver in the world.

The following story involved the miraculous and reveals how seafarers came to love Nicholas. It is only one of countless stories about sailors and ships that illustrates how Nicholas had a special affection "for those who go down to the sea in ships."

As did many young people in his times, Nicholas visited the Holy Land and prayed at the hallowed shrines in the footsteps of Jesus. Although the Holy Land was oppressed by Roman rule, many secret Christians in that region cared for the holy places. They took pilgrims into their homes and secretly guided them to the holy places.

After remaining several months with the Christian community in the Holy Land, Nicholas boarded a ship to return to Myra. During the first night at sea, Nicholas had a dream about the Devil's cutting the ropes that held the ship's main mast. Nicholas warned the captain and crew that they would be heading into a severe storm, He admonished them to pray so that all lives would be spared.

The storm lashed the boat, tossing it about as a tiny pea in the hand of a giant. Nicholas and all on board stormed Heaven with prayers. When the storm was at its fiercest the ship's first officer climbed the main mast to cut loose the ropes that held the sail in place. He lost his footing, fell to the deck and was instantly killed. He was found by his mates only after the storm had subsided.

The captain and crew approached Nicholas, reminding him that he predicted that no one would be lost. Nicholas asked that the dead officer be brought before him. Nicholas prayed over him and at once the first mate was restored to life. Fear and consternation seized all on board. The ship sailed smoothly on course and without further incident until it arrived at Myra.

The sailors accepted Nicholas as one of their own at the end of the voyage. At the same time, they were awed by the miracle they had witnessed. They gave him a nickname which, in time, almost came to be Nicholas' second name. Throughout the centuries sailors and countless other men and women invoked him by this name. They called him "Wonderworker."

For his own part, Nicholas returned to his uncle's monastery. He was penniless and now qualified for admission into the religious community. He continued his studies and made progress "in wisdom, age and grace." At the age of nineteen he was ordained a priest by his uncle, who by the closing year of the third century had become Bishop of Myra.

Scenes of the Life of St. Nicholas by Fra Angelico. (Top) The Birth of the Saint; His Vocation; His Gift of a Dower for Three Poor Maidens. (Bottom) Meeting the Imperial Messenger; Saving a Shipment of Grain for the City of Myra; Saving a Ship in Distress.

NICHOLAS THE BISHOP

CHANGES WERE BOTH MOMENTOUS AND MONUMENTAL IN the lives of men and women who lived at the turn of the fourth century in the Roman Empire surrounding the Sea in the Middle of the World. The Emperor Diocletian resigned his office in 305, thus bringing to an end that period in church history known as the Age of Martyrs.

Several years after Diocletian's resignation Constantine seized the imperial throne following the battle of the Milvian bridge in Rome in 313. Immediately he granted religious freedom to all the citizens of the Roman Empire. Christians were now free to worship the one, true God publicly, bringing about a blossoming of the Christian Church in the fourth century. The century is epitomized by such giants in the faith as the early Christian teachers, Saints Pope Leo the Great, Augustine of Hippo, Ambrose of Milan and Jerome of Jerusalem. Their wisdom enlightened the Church from then down to the present time.

During these early years of the century Nicholas of Myra entered into his manhood. Few, if any, who lived at that time realized that this Nicholas in the distant and poor province of Lycia would become better known and loved throughout the centuries than the shining intellectual lights among his contemporaries.

As the fourth century began, Nicholas was ministering to the early Christian people in and around Myra as their priest. Ancient records tell us that sometime during this period of his life he was also imprisoned with his fellow Christians and awaited the executioner's choice of the manner he would meet his death because of his Christian faith. Diocletian's resignation delivered him and countless other thousands of Christians throughout the empire from their dungeons.

Nicholas continued to minister as a priest among the people of Myra.

His ministry did not escape the notice of both the people and his superiors in the Church. His reputation had spread among the Christian community as the Wonderworker. People stood in awe at his gift of performing miracles, including the gift of healing. He was also noted as an exceptional teacher and eloquent preacher of the Christian faith.

One of the early biographers described in a strange sort of way the next major event in the life of Nicholas. The bishops of the Province of Lycia gathered in Myra to select a man to succeed his uncle, the old bishop, who was retiring because of infirmity and age. The election process dragged on until the bishops finally agreed that the first man who entered the church would be their unanimous choice as Bishop of Myra. At that moment Nicholas entered the church to give thanks to God for his safe return from one of his many ocean voyages. The bishops immediately placed the bishop's mitre on Nicholas' head.

Today the story seems a bit strange and exaggerated. The election of Nicholas as bishop needed no elaboration. Both his supernatural gift as a Wonderworker and natural gift of eloquence more than adequately endowed him as a bishop. Nicholas assumed the office of bishop in 313 A.D., shortly after the Emperor Constantine granted religious freedom to all the people in the Roman Empire.

By his calling, a bishop must bend every effort to strengthen and support the Christian faith among his people. Two incidents in his life reveal how deeply concerned Nicholas was with the Christian faith not only among his own people but throughout the entire known world. His first conflict was with a Greek goddess; the second with a living priest from Alexandria in Egypt. One involved hostile forces *outside* the Christian community; the other concerned false teaching *within* the Church.

Nicholas waged war against the Greek goddess, Artemis, in the center of his own city. Artemis, also known as Diana, whose statue in neighboring Ephesus was one of the Seven Wonders of the World, was most popular among the people of Asia Minor. In Greek mythology she was identified as the daughter of Zeus and the sister of Apollo. Artemis was the goddess to be invoked for many needs: she was goddess of the hunt, protector of animals, supplier of grain, protector of lovers. Her statues depicted her with many breasts because she was known as mother of all the living.

Such a powerful deity appealed to the simple minds of the pagan people throughout the Province of Lycia and in Myra. A colossal statue of Artemis stood in the central square of the city. Nicholas knew that the false worship of Artemis must be erased from the hearts and minds of the pagan people before the living Word of God would be able to take possession of their souls. So he set to work, first announcing the good news of the Gospel to anyone and everyone who would listen to him. His eloquence and learning led some of his listeners across the gap from paganism to Christianity. But not all.

All the best arguments in the world do not convince all the people in the world. Pascal wrote: "The heart has reasons which reason knoweth not." It often happens that symbols are more powerful than rational arguments.

The statue of Artemis in the city square kept her cult alive throughout the region. If the worship of Artemis was a hindrance to the presence of Christ Jesus – so Nicholas thought – then Artemis must disappear from the scene.

One night the citizens of Myra were awakened by a shattering noise that reverberated against the slopes of the surrounding mountains. The colossal statue of Artemis toppled from its pedestal. Christian men and women brought about her downfall. Some reported that Nicholas the bishop was present. Others said he assisted with his own hands in the actual destruction of the statue. Still others said he stood by, assisting by his prayers with what was considered an exceptional pious and good work of religion.

After that night of destruction the worship of Artemis declined in Myra and the surrounding area. Nicholas and his associates set about zealously in bringing former pagans into the one fold of Jesus Christ. In the first quarter of the fourth century the empire by the Sea in the Middle of the World witnessed a phenomenal growth in the number of Christian people. This phenomenon Nicholas and his associates also witnessed in Myra and the surrounding area.

No sooner had paganism been defeated, however, than another enemy of the Christian Church arose. This attack, however, came from within the community in the form of a distortion of the Gospels. This was recognized as heresy by some Christian leaders – but far from all. The proponents of this heresy followed the teachings of a priest in Alexandria, Egypt, who taught that Jesus Christ was not truly God but only *like* God. The teaching was insidious inasmuch as it undermined Christianity by denying the divinity of Christ and the existence of the Blessed Trinity. The priest who proposed this teaching was known as Arius and his heresy, to this day, is called Arianism.

The difference between the true and false doctrine depended upon two letters – the "i" and the "o." *Homoousios*, which means that Jesus is "of the same substance" of the Father and the Holy Spirit and *homoiousios* which means "of a similar essence."

The teachings of Arius spread throughout the Roman Empire, causing factions to form and even resulting in riots in many places. In those days Christians treated their religious beliefs very seriously, for as yet the world had not grown cold and indifferent to religious truth. Constantine the Emperor would not tolerate this divisiveness in his domain. He called all of the bishops of the Christian church to gather in the city of Nicea, across the Strait of the Dardenelles from the new city called Constantinople to replace Rome as the center of his administration. The emperor was more concerned about peace within the boundaries of the empire than with the

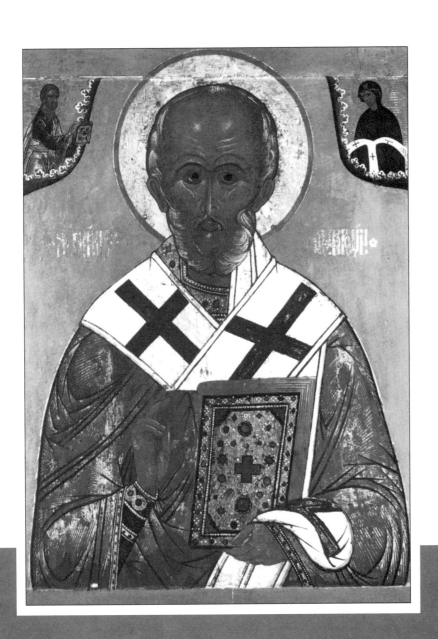

truth or untruthfulness of a teaching of the Christian faith. The peace of the empire – then as now – depended upon peace among Christian people.

Nicholas joined his brother bishops in traveling to Nicea in May, 325, to take his place as both a witness to and a teacher of the true Christian faith. This first ecumenical council of the Christian Church opened on May 20 and closed on June 19. The emperor presided over the assembly and the pope sent his representative.

During the assembly Arius, the priest from Alexandria, had the opportunity to state his teachings concerning the divinity of Christ. Damaskinos, a Greek monk living in Athens, described the scene in these words:

"The Emperor was now sitting on the throne, flanked by 159 bishops to his left and 159 to his right. Arius was presenting his views with great vigor and detail. As Saint Nicholas observed the scene, the Bishops listened to Arius in complete silence and without interrupting the discourse. Outraged, and prompted by his saintly vigor, he left his seat and walked over to Arius, faced him squarely and slapped his face.

"At this the assembly was shocked. Arius' supporters turned to the Emperor, asking that he intervene and punish Nicholas. They said, 'Oh, Just One, tell us, can it be fair that in your very presence someone should be permitted, without hindrance, to assault another? If he has anything to say in rebuttal, by all means let him have his say. But if he is not sufficiently learned to make a proper argument, then it were better if he remain in his seat quietly, and listen to others who are prepared to state their case in words.'

"Arius himself spoke directly to the Emperor, 'Should anyone who has the temerity to hit me, in front of Your Majesty, remain unpunished?' Emperor Constantine replied, 'Indeed, there is a law which forbids anyone to lift his hand in violence in the presence of the Emperor and it specifies that his hand be cut off. However, it is not up to me, in this Assembly, to act upon it. Instead, you, Your Holiness, should make the decision in this case; I leave it to your judgment, whether and how this act is to be punished.'

"The Bishops conferred with each other, and when they came to a decision, they said to the Emperor, 'Your Majesty, the Bishop of Myra has acted wrongfully. We all saw it happen and attest to it. We therefore ask your permission to let us strip him of his clerical garments, shackle him and place him under guard as a prisoner. In this way, he shall not be permitted to participate in the proceedings of the Council for the rest of our deliberations. Once the synod is completed, a final judgment in this case may be made.'

"As a result, that evening, Nicholas was made a prisoner in another wing of the Palace. He was placed in a a jail-like room, without his bishop's mantle and shackled on hand and foot. However, during the night he was visited by Jesus Christ and the Holy Mother. They observed Saint Nicholas in his cell and said, 'Nicholas, why are you imprisoned?' And Saint Nicholas said,

"Because of my love for you.' First they freed him from his shackles. And then Jesus said, 'Take this!' and he gave him a volume of the Holy Scripture. Then the Holy Mother went away, returned, and bought him his bishop's garments, so that he might clothe himself with appropriate dignity. At peace, he studied the Holy Book through the night.

"The next morning, a jailer came to bring him bread, saw that Nicholas was no longer shackled, that he was clothed in garments of his position, and that he was studying the Scriptures in his cell. Even his stole was in his one hand, while he held the book with the other. News of this miraculous event was quickly brought to the Emperor. He asked that Nicholas be freed, and when the two men met, the Emperor asked the Bishop's forgiveness."

The account of Nicholas' striking Arius seems authentic; the vision of Constantine is debatable. The fact that Nicholas was not punished for violating the rules of the Council gave rise, perhaps, to the invention of the vision by some pious writer. The story may also be the reason why Christian artists throughout the centuries have depicted Nicholas holding the Book of the Gospels in his right hand. So remarkable was this encounter between Nicholas and Arius that it was repeated, and embellished throughout the centuries more times than can be counted.

Nicholas displayed a vigorous, even violent, aspect of his character in both of these incidents, as well as others. These traits hardly seem to be a part of the kindly, loving and jolly patron of children we know today. A point must be made here in order to set the record straight.

Nicholas knew well the incident in the life of Jesus when he drove the moneychangers from the temple. He cast them from their stalls with a whip he had made, excoriating them for changing the Lord's house of prayer into a den of iniquity. Zeal for the truth also consumed Nicholas for he believed it was the Creed that mattered above all else as the basis for Christian faith. What a person believed determined how a person acted. Nicholas became the loving and beloved patron of children only because he was first adamantly committed to preserving the purity and integrity of Christian doctrine. Many artists have depicted Nicholas throughout the centuries with three golden balls somewhere in the painting. The three balls represent the three bags of gold that Nicholas threw through the window of the three maidens in distress.

Nicholas continued throughout the years as a bishop, dedicating his commitment to the material and spiritual welfare of the people whom he called his brothers and sisters. He loved them and they felt and returned his love. The Christian community in Myra flourished and its membership multiplied throughout the countryside. Nothing represented this mutual affection and assistance better than the many stories recorded about Nicholas and grain.

For the people who lived along the shores of the Sea in the Middle of the World, bread was not only the symbol but the very substance of life. Earthly bread sustained life in this world; eucharistic Bread was the pledge of eternal life in heaven. Nicholas broke both earthly and heavenly bread for his people. It is for this reason that so many of the stories told about Nicholas

The panel with the Virgin and Child between St. Nicholas (left) and St. John the Evangelist is by the 16th century artist Rico of Candia. It is inside the Basilica of St. Nicola in Bari, Italy (below). The church, built in the late 11th century, holds the mortal remains of St. Nicholas.

while he still lived on this earth have elaborated and multiplied over the centuries by biographers who wished to highlight Nicholas' love for his people.

One story tells of the time Nicholas stopped in the cottage of a poor family living in the foothills of the Taurus mountains. He invited himself to have supper with them. Deeply embarrassed, the father of the family protested, saying they had only a little bread left and even that would be insufficient for his family. Nicholas urged the good man to have confidence in God. Instantly Nicholas multiplied the grain in the bin and the family never suffered from lack of bread for the rest of their lives. Many variations on this story are recorded by many biographers.

Even more numerous are the stories about grain relating to the sea. Myra as a seaport was situated approximately midway between the imperial court in Constantinople and the grain fields of Egypt, whose major port was Alexandria. These stories all depict Nicholas not only as the deliverer of his people from famine (like the patriarch Joseph in ancient times) but also as the deliverer of their souls through the sacred bread made from the grain he brought to the docks at Myra.

One of the most delightful incidents concerning grain is told by Martin Ebon in his biography of Nicholas. He writes:

"There was a famine in Lycia, during which Bishop Nicholas frantically tried to obtain grain for the province. When several ships, on their way from Alexandria to Constantinople and loaded with grain, arrived in Andriaka, Nicholas hurried to the dock. He urged the captain of the ships to set aside a part of their load for Lycia. But the captain refused, saying that the loads had been weighed carefully and he would be held responsible for any shortages on delivery. However, the bishop assured him there would be no recriminations. He finally agreed to set aside one hundred bushels of grain from each ship. Miraculously, when the ships arrived at Constantinople, the grain weighed exactly what it had before. And when Saint Nicholas distributed the grain in Lycia, it lasted for two years, and there was enough left to serve as seed for future harvests."

In another of these stories Nicholas appeared to the captain of several grain ships on their way to Constantinople. He beseeched the captain to deliver to Myra some of the grain he carried and promised that he would be adequately recompensed and that not a single grain of his shipment would be lost. The captain realized a handsome profit from the exchange. In another story Nicholas appeared in the guise of a merchant to another captain aboard his grain ship at sea. This ship was destined to deliver its cargo to Rome for there the populace was suffering from an extreme famine. So also were Nicholas' people in Myra. He offered the captain three gold coins if he would drop anchor in Myra and unload some of his precious cargo of grain at the seaport. The captain was stunned three days later when, after dropping anchor in Myra, he recognized the "merchant" as Bishop Nicholas assisting in the distribution of the grain among his people.

Nicholas shepherded the Church of Myra for more than thirty years. His conspicuous love of children made him beloved by them, their parents and grandparents. All these years he was known as the Wonderworker and did not hesitate to invoke this exceptional gift from God to serve his people more effectively. In time he became one of those exceptional persons who become saints because they can never say "No," either to God or their neighbors.

In 344 the Angel of the Resurrection called Nicholas to his everlasting home. His body had been worn out by his labors; his spirit longed for that greatest moment in life – when Jesus embraces us with "an everlasting love."

After his death the priests and people buried his body in a small church in Myra. It immediately became a shrine and a place of pilgrimage. Nicholas continued to be in death the Wonderworker, even more so than when he was still in the land of the living. He was among the first of the saints to say, "I shall spend my heaven doing good upon earth."

NICHOLAS THE WONDERWORKER

THE MODERN MIND IS BAFFLED WHEN CONFRONTED BY miracles and legends, so evident when we consider Nicholas. People who live in this modern world like to think they have even the tiniest parcel of knowledge clarified, computerized and catalogued. They simply cannot do that with the transcendent virtues which are of true and lasting value in life.

The miracles that Nicholas performed cannot be catalogued because no one really knows how many he performed either in his life on earth or in Heaven. Even as a young man he was recognized as a Wonderworker when he restored life to the sailor who fell from the mast. His reputation as a Wonderworker grew throughout the centuries; in the retelling of the miracles attributed to him, people elaborated and embellished the stories.

This process of embellishment in time produced legends about Nicholas the Wonderworker. The few legends in this chapter are examples of those told in practically every language on the face of the earth. These stories are *not* just false stories. As legends they have an underlying truth at the heart of the story. The legend is rooted in reality. These stories, as preposterous as they may sound, enlarge upon a kernel of truth.

Nicholas, as we have seen, had the gift of performing miracles. Nicholas was not alone in possessing this gift. A man called Gregory was also a bishop who lived in Asia Minor. He died about a hundred years before Nicholas was born. He, too, was known as a Wonderworker. He shared this gift with Nicholas, just as other saints had other gifts such as converting pagans by the eloquence of their preaching, shedding tears profusely for the sins of mankind and healing the sick.

Most of us are familiar with legends. For example, there is the story of Paul Bunyan, the legendary lumberjack. Paul and his companion Babe the Blue Ox are the fiber of the legends that fueled the imaginations of millions of Americans during their growing-up years. Sooner or later the day comes when older and, presumably, wiser adults realize that all the stories about Paul Bunyan are legendary. That, however, does not in the least diminish the fact that once there was a lumberjack in the North Woods who performed prodigious feats in his career.

Miracles and legends are difficult for us to address because we live in a closing century which has wrought havoc with the Christian faith. Modern men and women that we are, we regretfully have entered a vacuum devoid of faith. The legends of Nicholas might just possibly restore our sanity, which presumes a modicum of reason, and with that restored, we might re-discover with the wonder of a child the depth and beauty of the mysteries of God.

The locale of the most numerous legends concerning Nicholas is the Sea in the Middle of the World. Nicholas loved seafarers and they, in turn, were devoted to him. The bonds of this mutual respect and reverence, admiration and affection, were first revealed, as we have seen, when the youthful Nicholas restored life to the sailor on the return journey to Myra from the Holy Land. No one has been able to keep a record of the stories that recount Nicholas' restoring life to countless seafarers who sought his intercession.

Another group of legends concerning seafarers concerns the actions Nicholas performed in safeguarding their ships in times of tempests and storms. Some of these legends record how the crew and passengers sought in prayer the intercession of Nicholas and their prayers were answered. Others tell how Nicholas appeared either in the heavens above or on the deck of the ship, giving the captain and crew directions on how to circumvent the storm-tossed sea. Another genre of these seafaring legends shows Nicholas in direct, personal combat with the devil. The artist, Albert Aldorfer, for example, depicted one of these legends in which the devil is bending the ship's mast to the breaking point and Nicholas is standing on the deck with his hand raised in exorcism.

In the course of the centuries, seafarers' affection for Nicholas prompted them to identify him as one of their own. They attributed to him the virtues – and even some of the more friendly customs – they exhibited themselves. Charles Jones records the following story in his biography of Saint Nicholas:

"Once all the saints were enjoying wine together. When the circulating cup reached Nicholas, he was too sleepy to hold it and let it drop. Saint Elias shook him by the arm to arouse him. 'O, I beg the company's pardon,' said Nicholas, 'but I have been very busy and was absent for your feast. The sea was rough, and I had to give my help to three hundred ships that were in danger. That is the reason for my being tired, and letting the cup fall out of my hands.'"

Nicholas had, without a doubt, a special affection for seafarers both as the Bishop of

Myra in this life and as their special patron in eternal life. He was recognized as the patron saint of seafarers long before – at least five or six centuries – he came to be regarded as the patron of children. Nicholas took special care of seafarers and they, in a sense of gratitude, were tireless in spreading his name and gift as a Wonderworker throughout the world.

This love of seafarers for their patron is reflected in several facts. There is not, even to this day, a major sea or river port in the world that does not have a church near the waterfront dedicated to St. Nicholas. Norsemen in the tenth century gave St. Nicholas' name to the first cathedral in the western hemisphere in Gardar, Greenland, in 1124. Christopher Columbus named several places in Florida for Saint Nicholas on his maps of exploration.

Throughout the centuries down to the present day Nicholas and seafarers continued a mutual love affair. One author noted, "All ships and boats carry his icon with an ever-burning lamp, and in his chapels models of boats, coils of cables, anchors, and such things are given as votive offerings." Jones makes this pertinent observation:

"Regularly in Greek ports... the church on the quay is dedicated to him. The newly discovered American shores were dotted with Saint Nicholas Ports, Saint Nicholas Ferries, and the like. Among the maritime protectors, only Santa Maria Stella Maris has been more generally invoked.... At La Pointe Saint-Nicholas, on the approach to the port of Moribhan in Brittany, sailors alternated the chant *Ave Maris Stellis* with prayers to Nicholas."

Nicholas the Wonderworker in his lifetime manifested his love for children and young people even before he boarded a ship. Incidentally, Nicholas is often depicted in religious art with three balls located beneath his feet or on a table near his side. In the course of the centuries confusion arose over the three balls. Some art critics interpreted these three balls to be the same as those that appeared on the coat-of-arms of the Florentine Medici, the wealthiest and most powerful banking family in medieval Europe. Following such mistaken identification pawnbrokers (who also use the three balls as their symbol) adopted Nicholas as their patron saint.

Legends concerning Nicholas' love for children, especially in the western Church, are more varied than those concerning seafarers. Nicholas assists young couples who desperately want children of their own. Nicholas helps women in travail safely deliver a new-born babe. Nicholas provides food for a poverty-stricken family whose children would die of starvation. Nicholas is ever present to serve all the needs of children in any dangerous situation in which they could be found.

Two legends among many are examples of Nicholas' love for children. The first, concerning three boys, was extremely popular in Europe; the other, concerning a lost boy, was favored in Asia Minor.

The legend of the three boys is the most bizarre and gruesome of all the stories about Nicholas' life. In some versions the three boys are described as college students; in others, seminarians studying for the priesthood. The core of the legend permitted the imagination of the storyteller free to run as wild as he or she desired. For this reason it was also the most popular of the miracle plays performed in city squares or in front of churches during the Middle Ages.

Incidentally, the number "three" in this legend, as in so many others, is in itself symbolic. "Three" took on a special religious significance following the Council of Nicea because its use, in itself, was a profession of faith in the Three Persons of the Blessed Trinity. Many icons show the one depicted with three fingers joined to recall the Blessed Trinity and two fingers joined signifying that Jesus is both God and Man.

One day Nicholas was traveling through the countryside which had been ravished by a famine that had afflicted the area for two years. Nicholas stopped in his journey at a roadside inn, seeking rest and nourishment. The innkeeper was deeply impressed by the importance of his guest, the Bishop of Myra. He provided him with the most comfortable lodgings he had and assured him that in a few hours he would have a delicious meal.

Nicholas came to the dining room in the inn, sat down at the table and awaited the fare the innkeeper promised. The bishop's suspicions were immediately aroused when the host provided a delicious stew. Nicholas inquired about the meat used in the stew and the proprietor said it was rabbit. This reply increased Nicholas' suspicions, for he asked himself how could rabbits survive in a wasted countryside that was not even able to provide sustenance for a chipmunk. He rose from his table and walked out of the dining room to inspect the kitchen.

He was angered by what he saw in the kitchen. Standing lined against the wall were three barrels filled with brine and containing the butchered members of what was obviously the bodies of three young men. The bishop was filled with compassion and immediately exercised his supernatural powers. By his command the dismembered bodies were joined together and the three young men stood before him in the full vigor of their youth. Nicholas reported the innkeeper to civil authority. The three young men proceeded on their way to school, singing the praises of God.

The legend of the three young men became one of the most popular in medieval Europe. Although the story is somewhat disconcerting, at least by the values we claim to espouse today, it portrayed to the medieval mind Nicholas as a most powerful patron of young people.

The other legend concerning Nicholas' intervention on behalf of children is more refined and more popular in the East than is the legend of the three young men. This is the legend of Adeodatus (which literally means "Gift of God") who lived in Myra seven centuries after Nicholas's death.

Adeodatus was the only child of an aged couple. They had prayed for many years that God would bless them with a child. When Adeodatus arrived the child filled the hearts of his parents with great joy. They loved him most dearly and he returned their love for him as a model of a devoted son. By the time Adeodatus reached the age of twelve a catastrophe struck his parents' home.

The fierce Turks had overrun Myra, captured many citizens, including Adeodatus, and

North European woodcut, from the Middle Ages, showing the saint as he reconstitutes the three students dismembered by the innkeeper. He is wearing his bishop's robes and carrying a mitre.

carried them off to Persia to be slaves. Adeodatus was taken into the home of a Muslim prince and served as cupbearer at his table. The day when Adeodatus and his companions were taken captive was the feast of Nicholas.

The youth's parents were overcome with sadness. Not a day passed that they did not shed bitter tears and lift their hearts and voices in supplication, asking Nicholas to intercede for them and bring about the safe return of Adeodatus. They never wavered in their belief that Nicholas would come to their aid.

One year to the day, again the feast of St. Nicholas, Adeodatus was standing beside his master's chair at the banquet table. Instantly he was lifted from his position and just as instantly he appeared at the front door of his parents' home in Myra. Everyone recognized that it was through the intercession of Nicholas that Adeodatus returned safely home.

The cult of Nicholas as patron of children was developed in the Western Christian Church, those countries in present-day Europe, earlier than in the Eastern Church, in Asia Minor and Russia. The custom of setting out shoes or stockings on the eve of Nicholas' feast seems to have originally developed in the Netherlands and later spread to other countries in Europe. St. Nicholas appeared in the village or the city, vested as a bishop of the Latin (not the Greek) rite, riding on a horse and assisted by a black servant. St. Nicholas was a Spanish bishop (for Holland was then subject to Spain) and his black servant was representative of the Moorish slaves in the Spanish dominion. The evolution of this Saint Nicholas to Santa Claus, embodying goodness and love, good cheer and virtue, heartiness and holiness was really not a difficult one, as we shall see.

Before his death in 344 Nicholas' reputation was established as a Wonderworker. Who would not overlook in later years his dropping a cup from his hand from sheer tiredness after saving 300 ships from ruin?

NICHOLAS THE TRAVELER

ICHOLAS WAS NOT A SAINT WHO KEPT HIS GIFTS HIDDEN under a bushel basket. He let his light shine, as we have seen, as a Wonderworker performing God's miracles for all who called upon him both during his life on earth as well as throughout the centuries from his home in Heaven. Throughout these years, as well as today, Nicholas has been a saint who traveled the highways of the world but also the lonely roads far removed from the beaten path. A heavenly mansion of pearls and gold was not to his liking; he would rather be on the road helping everyone in need.

Sailors, as we have seen, were his special friends. They launched Nicholas on his far-flung worldwide journeys; they made his name a household word in millions of homes throughout the world.

The two most important journeys of Nicholas became a reality only because of his friends, the seafarers. One of these journeys brought Nicholas to Kiev in the Ukraine; the other to Bari in Italy. Both journeys had a permanent impact on world culture and civilization.

In the eighth century the Vikings were the scourge of Europe. They were a mighty, bold and daring seafaring people from the northern lands of Europe who swept across a disorganized Europe following the collapse of the Roman Empire. The Vikings came to be called Northmen, or Norsemen, as they steered their long ships into the major seaports and riverports of Europe. They established a kingdom in Ireland; set one of their own on the English throne, founded a Norse, or Norman, Kingdom in southern Italy and so densely settled the northwestern part of France that to this day it is called Normandy. They pointed their long ships westward from Constantinople, establishing settlements in Iceland and Greenland and became the first Europeans to set their feet in what is now called North America. These same fearless seafarers took another route from their homeland in the north down the Dneiper River to present themselves as a fearsome and plundering scourge along the gates of Constantinople. Amazing accomplishments, indeed.

As these Norse traders sailed their ships up and down the Dneiper River they paused from place to place to establish trading and military posts along the route. One of these, Kiev, became a major center. Norsemen inter-married with the women of the native Slavic tribes, instilling a new vigor in these people and creating a new dynasty. These people, superior in the arts of navigation and warfare, became a constant fear and danger to the Byzantine Empire centered in Constantinople.

Olga, the princess-regent of Kiev, journeyed to Constantinople in 955 to became a Christian. She was royally received by both Patriarch and Emperor. Her grandson, Vladimir, halted the pirate raids on the emperor's city and embraced Christianity in 989. The emperor gave him the hand of his sister, Anna, the first royal princess ever to be given in marriage to a barbarian overlord. Upon his return to Kiev, Vladimir set to work bringing Christianity to the ancestors of the modern Russian and Ukrainian people. Unfortunately, most of Vladimir's conversions were made mostly by the persuasion of the sword. For this reason the patriarch of the Orthodox Church with his residence in Constantinople determined to eliminate this constant danger by sending Christian missionaries to bring the people freely into the fold of Christ. Thus the vast area in which the Ukrainian and Russian people lived in the tenth century came to be numbered among the followers of Christ.

Nicholas was no silent bystander observing the religious developments in this vast area. Seafarers carried his name and cult to Kiev. Christian missionaries pushed eastward, carrying the message of the Gospels to the tribes who ultimately joined together and became Russia. Again, seafarers carried the devotion of Nicholas to these people as they plied the waters of the Dneiper River.

One of the most curious travels of Nicholas brought him to Lapland, that land of snow surrounding the Arctic Circle in northern Europe and Russia. Missionaries from Moscow brought the Christian faith to these nomadic people whose survival depended upon the reindeer and whose economy was measured by the number of reindeer they owned. They lived in circular dwellings created from reindeer hides with a hole in the center to allow for the passage of smoke from the common fire in the center of the dwelling. This hole served as a chimney. The chief person in the tribe was the shaman, or medicine-man.

Among the Laplanders the shamans, or medicine men, took on mystical, almost supernatural, characteristics in the stories told about them during the centuries before they were

Christianized. These stories were embellished with the passage of time, as all stories tend to be. According to the stories, these medicine-men were extremely wealthy and had many reindeer. They were so powerful that at night they could get in their sleighs and their reindeer would drive them through the night sky wherever they wanted to go. And when they wanted to visit one of the tent-dwellings they descended the chimney, stepping out of their sleighs as the reindeer stopped in the middle of the sky. When these people accepted the Gospel of Jesus, their missionaries also encouraged in them a great devotion to Nicholas. So great was this cult of Nicholas that in time whatever the medicine-men could do, Nicholas could do, only much better and a lot more frequently.

One of St. Nicholas' biographers, Robin Chrichton, commented on this development:

"From the earliest days of Christianity, the policy of missionaries had always been to adapt and incorporate pagan customs by giving them a Christian interpretation and meaning. And the Arctic was no exception. Nicholas became a Super Shaman, a spiritual time-traveller, a mystic go-between for the people and their new Christian God. On his visits to the reindeer people, like the Shaman – and indeed everyone else – he came and went through the chimney – literally – in a cloud of smoke!"

In the course of time devotion to Nicholas became deeply rooted in the Christian soul of the Russian people. There in that expansive, sometimes mysterious, land called "Holy Russia," Nicholas received a status excelling even the honors he received from his native Asia Minor. After Jesus our Savior and Mary, the Mother of God, Nicholas exceeded all the other saints in the number of churches dedicated in his honor. The creators of icons – sacred images – brought their art to the consummate degree of excellence throughout the later years of the Middle Ages. Again, Nicholas was among iconographers' most popular image, following Jesus and His mother Mary. Finally, in most Russian homes during these centuries Russian boys and girls were taught to offer their prayers to the Heavenly Father with the conclusion "through Jesus Christ and Saint Nicholas."

A word about iconography is appropriate here. Most of the countless pictures of Nicholas are done in the style of Byzantine icons. The word "icon," coming from the Greek language, means "image." The ancient Christian artists did not want to paint ordinary pictures of Jesus and the saints, as the pagan artists had carved statues and painted pictures of their earthly rulers. The Christians, rather, tried to paint images that would attempt to go beyond the mere earthly looks of a person; they wanted to give some image of the inner reality, character, power and meaning of the person imaged that would lead the viewer beyond the earthly realm to heavenly or spiritual reality. God is holy, holy, holy, that is, beyond the earthly. So, too, Christ and His saints are holy, that is, beyond what human eyes could see.

Today there is a revival in the icon style of art, perhaps because many people are beginning to realize that "man does not live by bread alone." We need more, we need a spiritual dimension – we need God. Nicholas was a graced-tool of God and is now a part of that heavenly chorus praising the holy, holy, holy God.

Even almost a century of communist propaganda and domination could not erase devotion to Nicholas from the hearts of the Russian people. He remains today their most popular saint.

As seafarers took Nicholas northeastward in their travels, to Kiev in the Ukraine and Moscow in Russia, other seafarers, two centuries later, brought Nicholas northwestward through Bari to Italy.

Two provinces in Italy in the eleventh century were rivals for trade in the eastern part of the Sea in the Middle of the World. They were Venetia, with its capital, Venice, on the northern shores of the Adriatic Sea and Apulia, with its capital, Bari, further south. The two cities engaged in a sometimes acrimonious, and other times bloody, rivalry. Bari was particularly jealous because in the previous century Venice had acquired – by piracy, no doubt – the body of Mark the Evangelist from his shrine in Alexandria in Egypt.

At the beginning of the eleventh century the Roman Empire of the East, centered in Constantinople, was on the brink of total collapse. As a matter of fact, the fall of the magnificent city of Constantinople, center of law and order for more than seven centuries, fell to the onslaughts of the Turks in a decisive battle fought in 1073. Throughout this process of the disintegration of the eastern Roman Empire, the bodily remains of Nicholas laid buried in his tomb in the church dedicated in his honor in Myra. His resting place in so precarious a location caused not a little uneasiness in the hearts and minds of those who had a great devotion to him.

Seafarers, of course!

Those seafarers who brought Nicholas to Kiev and Moscow were descendents of the mighty Norsemen; these sailors in Bari were also descendents of the same stock. They were part of the Norman, or Norse, Kingdom in southern Italy. Creighton makes this observation:

"While half the armies of Europe were led by Norman soldiers, Norman sailors dominated the trade routes, maintaining links with the homelands but traveling to the extremities of the civilised world. Norman ships called at Myra and their crews came to hear of the reputation of St. Nicholas. Wherever they sailed they heard innumerable stories of how, against impossible odds, he had miraculously saved men from drowning and shipwreck. Ever since the miracle with the grain ships, St. Nicholas had been an increasingly important protector of sailors. What he could do for others, he could do for the Normans. Like so much else that they had made their own, the Normans accepted St. Nicholas as a powerful patron."

One day in 1057 a Norman captain and crew set forth from Bari on a special, unusual mission. To this day their motives have never become totally clear. Some say they sought to spare the mortal remains of Nicholas from the desecration that would certainly follow when the Turks came to Myra. Others say that they sought a saint more popular than Mark to be the patron of Bari.

Whatever the motives, after landing in the port of Myra they dressed as devout pilgrims on their way to the shrine of Nicholas. There they knelt piously in prayer before a handful of pilgrims and Orthodox monks who had charge of the shrine. Suddenly they unsheathed their swords, revealed the sledges and hammers concealed by their pilgrims' robes and set to work hastily. They excavated the saint's body and carried it off to their ship. More quickly than lightening flashes across the sky, their mission was accomplished.

A few weeks later, the ship entered the harbor at Bari amid the rejoicing of the local clergy and citizens. They now had a patron that rivaled and even excelled in importance the relics of St. Mark in Venice. They built a magnificent Norman basilica to enshrine the remains of this patron of seafarers and children. His presence brought prestige, honor and wealth to the southern port city on the Adriatic.

Sailors, whose methods and intentions may have been questionable, were responsible for making Nicholas one of the most popular saints in western Christendom as he already was in the eastern Church. This came about in another strange sort of way and was, again, made possible by seafarers, the special friends of Nicholas.

During the period of the Crusades, Bari became the second most important seaport for the embarkation of the soldiers of the Cross from every corner of Europe, carrying them to the Holy Land to defend the holy places. In Bari the crusaders became familiar with Nicholas and recognized him as a Wonderworker. Upon their return from the Crusades, they brought the name and reputation of Nicholas to their native lands. In a comparatively brief period of time, Nicholas attained the popularity in Europe which he had previously reached in Asia Minor and Russia. For several centuries, his shrine in Bari equalled, if it did not exceed, the popularity of the shrine of the Apostle St. James in Compostella, Spain.

Devotion to St. Nicholas spread like wildfire throughout Europe. Thousands of churches were dedicated in his honor in every country in Medieval Europe. Other people claimed him as a patron, such as pawnbrokers, children, students, women giving birth, farmers, and those unjustly accused who languished in jail. Such people turned to Nicholas to intercede for them with God. Nicholas' patronage of children, in the course of time, became the most popular.

The European mind was neither so formal nor serious as the mind of the East. Europeans, because of their faith, developed a certain whimsy in their life and thinking. Perhaps the novelist, Hilaire Belloc, put it best in a simple verse:

Wherever a Catholic sun doth shine,
There you'll find laughter and rich red wine.
At least I have always found it so –
Benedicamus Domino.

One of the most obvious differences between the eastern and western mind was the emphasis placed on the role of Nicholas in the lives of his devotees. In the East he was primarily the Wonderworker, performing marvellous and stupendous deeds. In the West he was the Giftgiver, revealing the generosity he manifested in his life upon earth to those who turned to him, especially children.

It seems this latter emphasis originated in Holland during the fifteenth century. At that time this tiny nation, created chiefly by damming up the North Sea, was known as Spanish Netherlands and subject to the Spanish Crown. A good and kindly Spanish bishop, assisted by his Moorish servant (later given the Germanic name of Ruprecht) appeared from time to time in Holland and distributed gifts and goodies to children. In time the Spanish bishop took on the popular image of Nicholas and the custom began of Nicholas' appearances in the squares of the cities and village of the Netherlands on the eve of his feastday, December 6. He usually entered and departed the square on horseback, pausing long enough to discover how well the children had learned their catechism.

That evening boys and girls set out their shoes by the doors of their houses or hung their stockings by the chimneys, awaiting a reward from Nicholas – whom they called Sankt Klaus in their native tongue. Good little boys and girls received a reward from the saint in the form of candies, cookies and fruit. Those who did not know their catechism and were naughty received a big black switch. Nicholas always knew if children were "naughty or nice."

The custom of giving gifts on the feast of Nicholas spread throughout Europe. Although the customs varied from country to country and even place to place, the underlying reason was the feast of Nicholas, the remarkable Wonderworker and Giftgiver. Without belief in and knowledge of Nicholas the saint, there would have been no such thing as giving and exchanging gifts throughout these centuries when the Christian faith was the foundation of European culture.

NICHOLAS THE DREAMER

AT THIS POINT IN OUR NARRATIVE WE WILL DIGRESS FOR a moment to include a poem by Charles A. Brady which appeared in the December, 1993, issue of *America*. Poets have a gift of expression which writers do not have. Charles A. Brady has that gift. He expresses in the following verse much of what I have been feebly trying to say in the preceding pages.

The great council was over. The bishop was weary.
Two months – and a week to travel – had left him homesick
For Myra, his see, and his own trundle bed.
Eight full weeks of wrangling about words!
Words he did not fully understand
Any more than most of the three hundred odd bishops
Who sat in mute conclave under Constantine,
Leaving the arguing to Alexander,
Spyridion of Cyprus, from Cordova Ossius.
And, most of all, Archdeacon Athanasius
Whose words winged upward as no one else's did.

One Word he did understand: the Word made flesh,
The Word the Father spoke when time was not:
And so he mastered the Greek formulas
Marking the hub of the mighty wheel that moved
this new thing under the sun, the Christian church's
First universal council in history.
Homooousios, *which meant consubstanial,*
Of the same essence with the Father, that is.
Homoiousios; *of like substance –*
One iota separated those words,
And, oh, what a difference that one iota made!
Like a jewelled dagger, envenomed, it struck home
And wounded the Incarnation mortally!
It robbed the Babe of his godhead with that I.
No longer would Omnipotence go swaddled.

Anger rose in Nicholas's breast as he remembered
That presbyter from Alexandria,
Arius, tall, dark, supercilious,
A popinjay of logic, skilled in reason
To fell the ivory tower of Mary's Child
With the battering ram of his accursed iota.
Particles were important, Matthew had said,
Defending jots and tittles in the Law.
Well, this yod was evil. It would destroy
The Nativity's great Feast of Little Things,

And Mary's Babe, the littlest thing of all,
Little Lord of the Birthing Feast that was so great.
Remember what the name, Nicaea, meant:
Victorious City; *and his name, Nicholas:*
Conquering Army, *the Bishop of Myra rose*
And smot the herisiarch on his learned nose.
Bright red it gushed before the labarum's *gold Chi-Rho.*
Constantine had a herald read aloud:
Ye servants of God, put away all cause of strife,
Unknot all discord in the Father's peace.

So the council ended in tumult, half-glad, half-sad.
Nicholas tossed and turned in the bed he would leave next morning,
Too tired to sleep, and too humiliated.
In July, the Emporer month, Nicaea was torrid.
No wind. The whining of mosquitoes only,
And the iron clank of camel gear outside.
His mind turned to his rustic see of Myra.
To the dowries he gave so that the maidens there
Might pay their lawful dues to a Christian eros.
To the children he served, his chosen apostolate.
He thought also of his single servant, Thorkel.
The man was a Northman, one of the northern soldiers
One came across here and there in the ranks of Caesar's legions.
A Christian now, he told amusing stories,
That Nicholas prized, about the old northern gods.

How hard it is not to sleep! A dream would be better.
Nicholas spoke aloud, from the Book of Job,
Words he loved in the Mass's Ordinary:
Your old men shall dream dreams,
           your young men shall
See visions. *Well, he was old enough for dreams,*
Wasn't he? Mirabile dictu! *It worked!*

As in all dreams, he woke. He woke in a sleigh
Cunningly carved into whorls and grinning faces.
He was a passenger. The charioteer
A brawny giant with a wild red beard
Who brandished an ancient hammer, and every time
Thunder roared all about. He was consubstantial –
The council's word still rang in Nicholas' head –
With the wildness of the night. The songs he sang,
In his barbaric northern tongue, were wilder yet.
The team he drove were goats, no horses at all.
It came into Nicholas's mind: here was Thorkel's god,
Thor of the Red Beard, wild hammer of heaven.

Somehow he wasn't afraid. Then that charioteer
Bowed with wild courtesy and handed him
The reins. Red beard streaming in the wind,
He was gone. And what a wind! The sleigh rode
on the wings of the wind. Like Isaiah's seraphim
That wind had six wings, white pinions of air,
Each one driving the sledge on, on, on.
And up! Up! The bishop was air-borne now,
High above the world below where other
Seraphim of snow, not air, robed trees
In glistening white surplices for
The Feast of the Baby God of Bethlehem.
Strangely enough – and yet it didn't seem strange!
Thor's goats were gone and, in their place, horned deer,
Their horns like candelabra to hold stars.
Thorkel had told him once these came from Lapland
Where the Sami pastured them on the Hyperborean
Marches of Norway. How they raced through the skies!
His sled – yes it was his sled now –
Had a curious cargo Myra's children would love:
Dolls, sweetmeats from Persia, toy helmets, horns.
Joy filled the heart of Nicholas at the sight,
Life and love and a giant's energy.
Faster and faster fell the natal snow,
Softer than baby cheeks or a kitten's fur.

The reindeer coursed through the night like the steeds of the gods.
A northern incense of firs fumed white on the air.

Nicholas woke in the dawnlight ruefully.
Sunt geminae Somni portae, *as Vergil wrote,*
Constantine's favorite poet. Sleep has two gates.
He knew what Constantine would ask.
          "Your dream,
Was it out of the Gate of Horn? Or of ivory?"
In a word, was it true or false? Nicholas sighed.

He couldn't ask Constantine. He was out of favor.
Besides, as a Celt, Vergil knew. Romans didn't.
He sighed once more. All he knew was this:
> *he'd like*
To have that dream again. Once every year.
Another sigh. He supposed he was getting old.

If Nicholas could have known, he really grew
> *young that night.*
As all the world grows young at Christmastide.
He didn't know then. We know, to our fortune,
> *however,*
All honor to St. Nicholas forever!
As it says in Paul's Epistle for his Mass:
He was a prelate, the end of whose teaching was
Jesus Christ yesterday, today, and the same forever.
He was not led away with any strange
> doctrine.
So Christmas is and stays our world's
> great dream.
And Nicholas' part therein? What shall one say?
Not alta fantasia, *no, Ah no,*
No matter how high that gift-sleigh's altitude.
A homlier fantasy, and most endearing,
The only tale of faery that's true.

NICHOLAS IN NIEUW AMSTERDAM

FOR ALL PRACTICAL PURPOSES, SAINT NICHOLAS AND Christmas were banished as holidays and holydays throughout northern Europe and Great Britain by the radical reformers, such as Oliver Cromwell. The feasts and accompanying festivities fared no better in the Colonies across the Atlantic.

Nicholas was barred from entering America by a law enacted by the Puritans of New England. The neighboring colonies, except Catholic Maryland, treated Nicholas and the Christ Child only a bit more kindly than the Bay Colony. In 1851, seeing that "popish trickery," that is, commemorating the feast of Saint Nicholas, was being observed in neighboring states, leaders of the Bay Colony put teeth into the law by attaching a fine to those who celebrated Christmas. Only in the present century has the sturdy stock of the Puritans' descendants stooped to celebrate the birthday of the Lord and recognize Santa Claus as St. Nicholas.

Colonists, mostly Protestant Waloons, sailed under the leadership of Cornelius May in 1624 to be the nucleus of the Dutch West India's colony in the New World. They settled on the tip of an island we now call Manhattan which Governor Piet Minuit purchased from the Native Americans for twenty-four dollars in beads and trinkets. Undoubtedly, this transaction was the most renowned in real estate history where the seller received so little and the buyer gained so much for so small an exchange. Minuit called his colony Nieuw Amsterdam.

This tiny colony survived no more than two generations before it was taken over by the English in 1664 and changed its name to New York. The Dutch colonists owned a good deal of

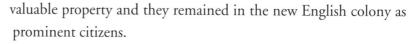

valuable property and they remained in the new English colony as prominent citizens.

The colonization of Nieuw Amsterdam was the occasion when Nicholas again became the subject of legends. Without a doubt, some of the colonists recalled the saint's annual visit from the days of their youth; even more recalled the candies, cookies and fruit he placed in their wooden shoes and stockings. A few, perhaps, from the older "Catholic days," may have remembered that Nicholas was the Bishop of Myra who had a popular shrine in Bari, Italy, and was especially the patron of boys and girls.

The colonists who settled in Nieuw Amsterdam were fully aware of the law in their native land concerning Nicholas. Most of them resented the ordinance which read, in part:

"Since the magistrates have learned that in previous years, notwithstanding the publishing of the Bylaws, on Saint Nicholas Eve various persons have been standing on the Dam and other places in the town with candy, eatables, and other merchandise, so that a large crowd from all over town gathered, ...the same magistrates, to prevent all such disorders and to take the superstition and fables of the papacy out of the youths' heads, have ordered, regulated, and opined that on Saint Nicholas Eve no persons, whoever they may be, are to be allowed on the Dam or any other places and streets within this town with any kind of candy, eatables, or their merchandise...."

In other words, the magistrates were "Scrooges" two centuries before Charles Dickens created the character in *A Christmas Carol*! These magistrates proved to be the Grinches who stole Christmas, to use the imagery of a modern fable. That took care of Nicholas' making the rounds on the eve of his feast or on Christmas eve.

Another custom concerning Nicholas somehow seemed to have survived in this new Dutch colony. In the high Middle Ages bakers in the larger cities of Europe created Nicholas cookies. These were elegant and sumptuous creations, stamped with the image of Nicholas dressed in his episcopal pontificals, similar, as an art form, to the exquisite Easter eggs exchanged among the Ukrainian and Russian people at Easter time. Nicholas cookies were exchanged among business associates, neighbors and members of the family. A bottle of brandy or some cordial often accompanied the gift.

The forms for making Nicholas cookies seemed to have survived the fury of the radical reformers during the Reformation. Nicholas cookies were shipped from Antwerp – a center of Catholicism – to the colonists in Nieuw Amsterdam. This custom was practiced by adults

"Seeing Santa Claus," by Thomas Nast. From Harper's Weekly, *January 1, 1876.*

although, as Washington Irving noted, principally on New Year's Day rather than either the feast of Saint Nicholas or Christmas:

"In his days, according to my grand-father, were first invented those notable cakes, new-year cookies, which originally were impressed on one side with the honest burly countenance of the illustrious Rip Van Dam; and on the other with that of the noted St. Nicholas, vulgarly called Santeclaus; – of all the saints of the calendar the most venerated by true Hollanders, and their unsophisticated descendants. These cakes are to this time given on the first of January to all visitors, together with a glass of cherry-bounce or raspberry brandy."

Apart from this reference to Nicholas cookies by Irving, the most popular account of Saint Nicholas in Nieuw Amsterdam was recorded by a New York historian, Mary L. Booth, in her book, *History of the City of New York*, which was published in 1859. She wrote:

"The Dutch had five national festivals which were observed throughout the city, namely, Kerstrydt (Christmas); Nieuw jar (New Year); Paas (the Passover); Pinx (Whitsunide); and Santa Claus (St. Nicholas or Christkinkle day)... but Santa Claus day was the best of all in the estimation of the little folk, who of all others, enjoy holidays the most intensely. It is notable, too, for having been the day sacred to St. Nicholas, the patron saint of New York, who presided at the figure-head of the first emigrant ship that touched her shores, who gave his name to the first church erected within her walls, and who has ever since been regarded as having especial charge of the destinies of his favorite city. To the children, he was a jolly, rosy-cheeked little old man, with a low-crowned hat, a pair of Flemish trunk-hose, and a pipe of immense length, who drove his reindeer sleigh loaded with gifts from the frozen regions of the North over the roofs of New Amsterdam for the benefit of good children. Models of propriety were they for a week preceding the eventful Christmas eve."

This is the story that members of the older generation learned in their childhood about the coming of Nicholas to America. For almost one hundred and fifty years American school children were taught this account. Mary Booth wrote this account in 1859, exactly one hundred and ninety-five years after the Dutch surrendered their colony to the British, who named it New York. A contemporary historian, Charles W. Jones, in his fascinating and sometimes cynical biography, *Saint Nicholas of Myra, Bari, and Manhattan*, made an exhaustive study of Booth's account. He stated his conclusion in these no uncertain terms:

"When we look at the available documents – that is, newspapers, magazines, diaries, books, broadsides, music, visual aids, and merchandise of the past – Miss Booth appears to have been correct in only one particular, that the cult of 'Santa Claus' originated in New York City, from which it spread. There was no Nicholas or Christkinkle Day, no patron saint of New Amsterdam or New York, no figurehead of Nicholas on an emigrant ship, no dedication of the first church to *any* saint, no iconography, no pipe, reindeer, or North."

Jones further pointed out that the earliest record of St. Nicholas in the New York colony was recorded in *Rivingon's Gazetteer* on December 23, 1773 – almost one hundred and fifty years after the Dutch came to the new world: "Last Monday the anniversary of Saint Nicholas, otherwise called St. a Claus, was celebrated at Protestant Hall, at Mr. Waldron's, where a great number of Sons of that ancient Saint celebrated the day with great joy and festivity."

Another reference Jones cited indicates that the cult of St. Nicholas was later flourishing in New York. The same journal carried the following notice on December 8, 1774: "Monday next, being the anniversary of St. Nicholas, will be celebrated by the descendants of the ancient Dutch families."

In such a way legends are made! As we have seen, Nicholas had been the subject of countless legends in his lifetime and throughout the centuries. One can hardly be surprised that the New World should clothe Nicholas with legends from the earliest years of its colonization. Although Jones offers convincing evidence for his denial of the facts that Booth records, it is this writer's belief that Booth's story, and not Jones' rational arguments, will survive in the course of time.

Another writer in New York did, however, preserve Saint Nicholas and Christmas for future generations. Jones rightly states that the author, Washington Irving, is chiefly responsible for this survival. His name became associated with Saint Nicholas when he was proposed as a possible member of the New York Historical Society in 1809. At the meeting of the society that year the toastmaster made this toast: "To the memory of Saint Nicholas. May the virtuous habits and simple manners of our Dutch ancestors not be lost in the luxuries and refinements of the present time."

One can only imagine how loud the guffaw would have been from Irving if he had not politely suppressed it. He spent a considerable amount of time in writing *The Knickerbocker History* to create a satire of "the virtuous habits and simple manners" of the Dutch descendants of the original colonists. In that work Washington Irving mentions Santa Claus and Saint Nicholas twenty-two times. In such a way he kept alive the memory of the former Bishop of Myra and patron saint of children.

In the same work he explained his reason for writing his history, stating that many of his fellow-citizens never knew "...that New York had ever been called New Amsterdam, or had heard of the names of its early Dutch governors or cared a straw about their ancient Dutch progenitors.... The main object of my work... was to embody the traditions of our city in an amusing form; to illustrate its local humors, customs, and peculiarities, to clothe home scenes and places and familiar names with those imaginative and whimsical associations so seldom met within our new country, but which live like charms and spells about the cities of the Old World, binding the heart of the native inhabitant to his home."

The future of Santa Claus was assured in New York by 1810 through the efforts of Washington Irving and a handful of associates. Although his presence was not widely known among the colonists of British descent who had lost the image and role of the saint in their collective memory, there were enough to assure its preservation. In 1811 there existed at least one testimony of this in an anonymous verse that appeared "east side, west side, and all around the town":

Oh good holy man! whom we Sancte Claus name,
The Nursery forever your praise shall proclaim:
The day of your joyful revisit returns,
When each little bosom with gratitude burns,
For the gifts which at night you so kindly impart
To the girls of your love, and the boys of your heart.
Oh! come with your panniers and pockets well stow'd,
Our stockings shall help you to lighten your load,
As close to the fireside gaily we swing,
While delighted we dream of the presents you bring.

Oh! bring the bright Orange so juicy and sweet,
Bring almonds and raisins to heighten the treat;
Rich waffles and dough-nuts must not be forgot,
Nor Cullers and Oley-Cooks fresh from the pot.
But all these fine presents your Saintship can find,
Oh! leave not the famous big Cookies behind.
Or if in your hurry one thing you mislay,
Let that be the Rod — and oh! keep it away.

Then holy Saint Nicholas! all of the year,
Our books we will love and our parents revere,
From naughty behavior we'll always refrain
In hopes that you'll come and reward us again.

NICHOLAS IN OLD NEW YORK

SEAFARERS THROUGHOUT THE CENTURIES, AS WE HAVE seen, have been the special friends of Nicholas. Artists and writers, however, have not been too far behind in showing favor to the patron saint of children.

In the eastern Orthodox Churches, Nicholas has been one of the favorite subjects of the icon-makers. These men (for it was not a calling open to women) were primarily monks who lived in monasteries. They were expected by both the officials and lay members of the Church to strive sedulously to imitate the holiness of the Lord, the Mother of God and the saints they depicted in their art. Icons depicting Nicholas and his life are scattered throughout the churches of the Ukraine and Russia; some are deposited in the famous Russian art museum in St. Petersburg.

In the West, in both the Catholic and Protestant Churches, artists also found Nicholas and the legends surrounding his life a popular subject of their works. Blessed Fra Angelico is only one among thousands of artists in this group. Works of many of these masters are found in most of the major art museums of Europe.

Libraries throughout the world hold books about Nicholas, his life and his influence. Almost every Christmas-tide a booklet about Nicholas, such as this one, appears in print in one corner of the world or another. Editors of publications would be considered remiss in their duties if they did not encourage some sort of written or graphic feature commemorating Nicholas. This practice was more lavish and expansive in the past, but the practice still continues.

In the United States, three men emerged in the nineteenth and twentieth centuries to make Nicholas more popular among both churchgoers and non-churchgoers. Two of these were New Yorkers. Clement Clark Moore was an Episcopal clergyman; Thomas Nast was a political cartoonist. The third man, Haddon Sundblom, lived in Chicago during the early and middle years of this century. Although other artists and writers made Nicholas the subject of their works, these three men had the greatest impact in transforming the image of Saint Nicholas into the Santa Claus we know today in American society.

At the beginning of the nineteenth century Clement Clark Moore was a wealthy and influential clergyman who lived "far from the madding crowd" of New York City which at that time was a cluster of wooden and brick buildings hanging on to the tip of Manhattan Island with church steeples and windmills the only major edifices piercing the skyline. He, his wife and six children lived in a huge, rambling mansion in a district called Chelsea, an area in the city today between Eighth and Tenth Avenues and West Nineteenth and Twenty-fourth Streets. The Reverend Mr. Moore was one of the founders of New York General Theological Seminary and there served as professor of Oriental and Greek Literature. He was recognized as a distinguished scholar following the publication of his Hebrew dictionary and other works.

Clement Moore may have been distinguished in learned and religious circles; in the mansion he inherited from his grandfather he was a model family man who enjoyed most of all being with his children. On special occasions, such as their birthdays, Easter, Christmas, New Year's Day, he composed verses for them and enjoyed reading his verses to them and the company who joined the family on these holidays. In 1822 he composed a lengthy verse which he entitled "A Visit from St. Nicholas."

The verse might well have been consigned to the waste-basket as many other verses of Moore had been. However, one of those twists which often make fact stranger than fiction occurred in the Moore household on Christmas day in 1822. A friend of the family listened as the clergyman read his verse. She liked it, copied it and took it home with her. She, in turn, showed it to relatives and friends, who in turned copied it. One of these was a Sunday School teacher who sent it to her local newspaper. On December 23, 1823, the poem appeared in the *Troy Sentinel*. From that year to the present, the poem has been reprinted more than any other piece of writing in the United States.

The editor of the up-state New York newspaper published Moore's poem under these introductory remarks: "We know not to whom we are indebted for the following description of

that unwearied patron of Children – that homely but delightful personification of parental kindness – Santa Claus, his costume and his equipage; as he hops about visiting the firesides of this happy land, laden with Christmas bounties, but from whomsoever it may have come, we give thanks for it." Later in life Moore was proud to acknowledge authorship of the poem and had it published in a collection of some other verses.

No book about Saint Nicholas would be complete without Moore's poem as he had originally composed it.

A VISIT FROM ST. NICHOLAS

'Twas the night before Christmas when all through the house
Not a creature was stirring, not even a mouse;
The stockings were hung by the chimney with care,
In hopes that St. Nicholas soon would be there;
The children were nestled all snug in their beds,
While visions of sugar-plums danced through their heads;
And Mamma in her kerchief, and I in my cap,
Had just settled our brains for a long winter's nap –
When out on the lawn there rose such a clatter,
I sprang from my bed to see what was the matter.
Away to the window I flew like a flash,
Tore open the shutters and threw up the sash.
The moon, on the breast of the new-fallen snow,
Gave a luster of mid-day to objects below,
When what to my wondering eyes should appear
But a miniature sleigh, and eight tiny reindeer,
With a little old driver, so lively and quick,
I knew in a moment it must be St. Nick.
More rapid than eagles his coursers they came,
And he whistled, and shouted, and called them by name;
"Now, Dasher! now, Dancer! now, Prancer and Vixen!
On, Comet! on, Cupid! on, Dunder and Blitzen –
To the top of the porch, to the top of the wall!
Now, dash away, dash away, dash away all!"
As leaves that before the wild hurricane fly,
When they meet with an obstacle, mount to the sky,
So up to the house top the coursers they flew,

"'Twas the night before Christmas, when all through the house
Not a Creature was stirring, not even a mouse"
       (The final picture in Harper's Weekly. *From the original drawing.)*

With a sleigh full of toys – and St. Nicholas, too.
And then in a twinkling I heard on the roof
The prancing and pawing of each little hoof.
Down the chimney St. Nicholas came with a bound.
He was dressed all in fur from his head to his foot,
And his clothes were all tarnished with ashes and soot;
A bundle of toys he had flung on his back.
And he looked like a peddler just opening his pack.
His eyes how they twinkled! his dimples how merry!
His cheeks were like roses, his nose like a cherry;
His droll little mouth was drawn up like a bow,
And the beard on his chin was as white as the snow.
The stump of a pipe he held tight in his teeth,
And the smoke, it encircled his head like a wreath.
He had a broad face, and a little round belly,
That shook when he laughed, like a bowl full of jelly.
He was chubby and plump – a right jolly old elf;
And I laughed when I saw him, in spite of myself.
A wink of his eye, and a twist of his head,
Soon gave me to know I had nothing to dread.
He spoke not a word, but went straight to his work,
And filled all the stockings, then turned with a jerk,
And laying his finger aside his nose,
And giving a nod, up the chimney he rose.
He sprang to his sleigh, to his team gave a whistle,
And away they all flew like the down of a thistle;
But I heard him exclaim, ere he drove out of sight,
"HAPPY CHRISTMAS TO ALL AND TO ALL A GOOD NIGHT!"

The second nineteenth century individual who advanced the popularity of Nicholas was Thomas Nast, an artist and illustrator whose work found a home in New York newspapers and in such journals as *The Atlantic Monthly*. He was one of the many immigrants who enriched and enhanced the United States by using the talents they brought with them from the Old Country. A native of Bavaria, he emigrated with his parents when he was very young. He was not distinguished as a student but, spending most of his time in developing his artistic ability during his school years, he did, at least, earn the grudging approval of his teachers.

Nast entered upon a career of a political cartoonist. His work was widely followed and commented upon not only by New Yorkers but political leaders throughout the country. He was outspoken in his political views and thus was disliked, perhaps, more than he was liked. He received as a political plum from President Theodore Roosevelt the office of U.S. consul in Quayaquil, Ecuador. There, after serving in his country's diplomatic service less than a year, he died of malaria in 1902.

The private life of Nast, however, was an entirely different matter. He was a family man, preferring to be in the company of his wife and children rather than artists and politicians.

"The Christmas spirit," wrote Nast's biographer, Albert Paine, "was always a distinct element in Nast's work and a mighty influence in his household." Paine, writing about the artist's position in 1876, added:

"At the door of the now prosperous Nast household Christmas purchases were delivered in relays far into the dusk of Christmas Eve, and these the happy parents took a vast delight in arranging in an original and unconventional manner to make glad the brood of early risers on Christmas Morning.... There was always a multitude of paper dolls – marvellous big and elaborate paper dolls – a race long since become extinct. And these the artist father – more than half a child himself at the Christmas season – arranged in processions and cavalcades, gay pageants that marched in and about those larger presents which could not be crowded into the row of stockings along the studio mantel. It was a time of splendor and rejoicing – the festive blossoming of the winter season – and it was a beautiful and sturdy family that made merry Christmas riot in the spacious home."

Nast's political interests and activities ceased as soon as he crossed the threshold of his home. The artist who made Moore's poem come to life in the imaginations of millions of people remained a child in a corner of his heart. For this reason he produced the amazing number of forty-five illustrations of Saint Nicholas, or Santa Claus, in his career. His works appeared in *Harper's Weekly* for more than thirty years; his last contribution to that publication being another illustration of "A Visit from St. Nicholas."

In the course of the years Nast's illustrations of Santa Claus varied until, finally, they arrived at a fixed maturity. In the course of time the Gift-Giver exchanged his episcopal robes for a red and furry suit. The visitor "who spoke not a word, but went straight to his work," came to look exactly as Moore described him:

> His eyes how they twinkled! his dimples how merry!
> His cheeks were like roses, his nose like a cheery;
> His droll little mouth was drawn up like a bow,
> And the beard on his chin was as white as the snow.

1936

1949

"Sundblom Santa"

The late Haddon Sundblom helped create today's universally recognized image of Santa Claus through a series of popular holiday advertisements for The Coca-Cola Company.

Thomas Nast St. Hill, grandson of the artist, published the forty-five drawings of Santa Claus in a book entitled *Thomas Nast's Christmas Drawings*. He wrote: "The learned American professor and Thomas Nast, the young German-born artist, gave the world a new image of St. Nicholas and one that would live in the hearts of children for generations to come."

Most readers would agree with St. Hill when he wrote that without his grandfather's drawings "the St. Nicholas described by Moore's pen might never have survived." It is noteworthy, for our purpose here, to emphasize that both Moore and Nast recognized Santa Claus as just another name for Saint Nicholas. The commercialization of Santa Claus was brought about by another artist working in the twentieth century.

Haddon Sundblom was a Swedish-American who lived in Chicago in the first half of the twentieth century. In 1931 the Coca-Cola Bottling Company commissioned him to draw a painting of Santa Claus. Between 1931 and 1966 Sundblom painted Santa Claus thirty-five times for Coca-Cola. In the latter years he used himself as his model.

Sundblom's Santa included several additions to Nast's portrayal. The former's Santa was taller and more American in the features of his face. Sundblom also was not reluctant to place his Santa Claus in several mischievous situations, such as raiding the refrigerator, playing with the family's puppy, and slipping an extra orange into a stocking. In many of these paintings Sundblom's Santa holds a bottle of Coca-Cola in his hand. The image of Santa Claus that most Americans have today is Sundblom's, not Nast's.

Robin Crichton makes this indictment:

"It was Coca-Cola who really exploited Santa's commercial potential. At Christmas in 1931 Santa Claus was shown swigging from a bottle of Coca Cola on billboards, in magazines, and on shop counters all over the States. Wherever Coca Cola was being sold in the world, Santa Claus was there to promote it, and continued to do so every Christmas for the next thirty-five years."

Fortunately, the innocence of children prevented them from being aware of the commercialization of their patron. In spite of Coca-Cola, they could still sing:

> Jolly old Saint Nicholas,
> Lend your ear this way.
> Don't you tell a single soul
> What I'm going to say.

In the latter half of the nineteenth century magazines on both sides of the Atlantic Ocean carried each year household hints for celebrating Yuletide. Some of these suggestions were:

❄ "See that there is abundance of Christmas literature about. Servants and children as well as the grown-up guests delight in looking at pictures....

❄ "The one ingredient to be universally infused is gladness. Everyone can, at all events, endeavor to bring goodwill and a smiling countenance to the festive board, banishing for a time the recollection of everyday worries.... This is especially the children's time and we would have them as happy as we were in the old Christmas Days of long ago....

❄ "It is worthwhile to bestow some little trouble on the decoration of the rooms. Have plenty of shining holly, and laurel too, and don't omit the mistletoe, for we have long ago forgotten all about the paganism, magic and superstition which surrounded it....

❄ "Presents are inseparably connected with the season.... There are two points to be considered – first, what to give, and then how best to make the giving a source of pleasure."

As Clement Moore's poem left its mark on American readers, Charles Dickens and other writers were doing the same in England.

Dickens' descriptions of Christmas festivities in Dingly Dell and the Christmas dinner in Bob Cratchit's home struck responsive chords in the hearts of English and American readers. More discriminate readers felt Sir Walter Scott's description of Christmas in *Marmion* a better portrayal of the festive day in past ages. Scott's introduction to Canto VI opened with these lines:

> On Christmas eve the bells were rung;
> On Christmas eve the mass was sung:
> That only night in all the year,
> Saw the stoled priest the chalice rear.
> The damsel donn'd her kittle sheen;
> The hall was dress'd with holy green;
> Forth to the wood did merry-men go,
> To gather in the mistletoe.
> Then open'd wide the Baron's hall
> To vassal, tenant, serf, and all;
> Power laid his rod to rule aside,
> And Ceremony doff'd his pride.

By the end of the nineteenth century Saint Nicholas as Santa Claus was restored in the countries of northern Europe and found a congenial home in the United States. Once again he was filling the hearts of millions of children with joy.

NICHOLAS AND HIS CHILDREN

IN THE CENTURIES FOLLOWING HIS ENTRANCE INTO HEAVEN, Nicholas was honored primarily as the Wonderworker. In the thirteenth century, however, almost exclusively in the western Church in Europe, Nicholas began being honored primarily as a Gift-giver. This came about in almost a casual, offhand manner.

It seems that the custom originated in France in the twelfth century. Nuns chose the eve of the feast of Saint Nicholas to visit stealthily and secretly the homes of poor families, leaving at their doorsteps oranges, cakes and candies. It was only a matter of time when others imitated the example of the nuns and concentrated their good deeds chiefly on the children of these poor families.

The verse might well have been consigned to the wastebasket as many other verses of Moore had been. However, one of those twists which often make fact stranger than fiction occurred in the Moore household on Christmas Day in 1822. A friend of the family listened as the clergyman read his verse. She liked it, copied it and took it home with her. She, in turn, showed it to relatives and friends who in turn copied it. One of these was a Sunday School teacher who sent it to her local newspaper. On December 23, 1823, the poem appeared in the *Troy Sentinel*. From that year to the present, the poem has been reprinted more than any other piece of writing in the United States.

Gift-giving thus became associated with Saint Nicholas. These customs were brought to the United States chiefly by religious teachers. They continued to be practiced in private and parochial schools, especially in those areas where the population was heavily Catholic or German Lutheran. Stearns County, Minnesota, has been one of these centers.

Mrs. Elsie Hellerman of rural Melrose, Stearns County, recalls the visit from Saint Nicholas in her younger years:

"When I was a young girl in the 1920s I lived on a farm in rural Melrose and attended a rural country school. In song-time in school there were always songs of the season. On the day before the feast of Saint Nicholas we always sang 'Jolly Old St. Nicholas.'

"The teacher then admonished us to be good boys and girls. She said Saint Nicholas was watching us to see if we were naughty or good. She also told us to obey our parents always. This made me think of what Saint Nicholas would tell me, or ask me, when he came to our house that night.

"I rushed home especially on that day. I carried in the wood to fill the woodbox in the kitchen. I hurried out to the barn to milk the same cows I milked every morning and evening. I returned to the house and set the table for supper.

"During supper our parents asked us whether or not we had been good because St. Nick would ask us when he came. This got me thinking about what questions he would ask me.

"We cleaned the dishes and waited…and waited. Someone suggested that we might sing some songs so St. Nick could find us.

"After a while, which seemed like eternity, there was a 'tap – tap – tap' on the window. As children we all looked at each other with wonderment in our eyes. Next – a knock on the door.

"St. Nick walked in, shouting 'Ho! Ho! Ho!' He was dressed in red with a bag slung over his shoulder and he carried a stick in his hand.

"'Have you been a good little girl?' He was standing in front of me and my heart was beating louder than a drum. He looked around at my three brothers and sister. He asked us to recite our prayers. I was scared stiff.

"He asked all of us to sing a song and he directed us with his stick. When we were finished he opened his bag and pulled out candies and nuts for all of us.

"St. Nick left with a 'Ho! Ho! Ho!' We all sat around the table, enjoying the goodies he left. I could not wait until he would return next year."

The custom of giving gifts to children on the eve of Nicholas' feast, however, gradually declined in America. Already by the time Moore wrote his poem the appearance of Saint Nicholas (Santa Claus) was scheduled for Christmas Eve or Christmas Day in most areas of the United States.

Santa Claus is ubiquitous in the United States today. He comes early on television and in department stores (most people would say too, too early), and is again the victim of greedy exploitation. He stands on street corners ringing a bell and the passers-by wonder if he is really ringing his bell to help the poor or is a phony only trying to line his own pockets. He is the main attraction in Macy's annual parade on Thanksgiving Day. One year he was deeply embarrassed when he rose from his chair to wave his hands at his devoted followers – and his trousers dropped to his ankles! Another year in Los Angeles he became the victim of an all too ardent child who sat on his knee. The boy took a heavy metal toy he carried in his hand, raised it high and put a dent in Santa's skull. Santa maintained a pleasant smile and asked the child why he did that. The boy replied, "You didn't give me what I asked for last year."

Another phenomenon associated with Santa Claus was the establishment of a town in Indiana named Santa Claus. Each year the post office is flooded with letters to Santa, making the employment of additional Postal workers a necessity. Playing the role of Scrooge, the United States Postal Service announced that it was going to eliminate the post office in Santa Claus, Indiana, because of the extra expense at Christmas-time. A hue and cry arose throughout the nation. The post office remained open and Santa Claus is assisted by a group of faithful volunteers in answering letters. Each year the post office receives more than fifteen thousand letters to Santa. This is one it recently received:

"Dear Santa:

"We live in Minnesota. Our name is on the mailbox. You go straight down, then you go left and then right and then, straight up ahead. Our house is all white with green trim on it, but please, Santa, do not put another frozen frankfurter in my stocking this year.

Mary Jo."

Undoubtedly, the most famous letter concerning Saint Nicholas was written in 1897. The writer was a little girl named Virginia O'Hanlon who lived in New York City. Some of her schoolmates told her that there was no Santa Claus; she asked her father, and he was evasive on the subject. She addressed a letter to the Question and Answer column in the *New York Sun* newspaper. She wrote:

"Some of my little friends say there is no Santa Claus. Papa says 'If you see it in the *Sun*, it's so. Please tell me the truth, is there a Santa Claus?"

In another of those situations where fact is stranger than fiction the girl's letter was passed from the Question and Answer desk to Frank Church's desk. At first sight, he would have appeared to be the last man in the world qualified to answer Virginia's question. He had served as a Civil War correspondent for the *New York Times* and was hardened and cynical by such experience. The same newspaper described him as "a man of sardonic bent whose personal motto was, 'Endeavor to clear your mind of cant.'" Such was the man, Frank Church, who perhaps wrote the best known and most enduring editorial in the annals of American journalism. The editorial was re-printed each Christmas season in the pages of the *Sun* and other newspapers for more than half a century. It was not known until some time after his death on April 11, 1906, that Church was the author of the editorial.

The piece appeared on September 21, 1897, under this headline and read as follows:

YES, VIRGINIA, THERE IS A SANTA CLAUS

Virginia, your little friends are wrong. They have been affected by the skepticism of a skeptical age. They do not believe except they see. They think that nothing can be which is not comprehensible by their little minds.

All minds, Virginia, whether they be men's or children's, are little. In this great universe of ours man is a mere insect, an ant, in his intellect, as compared with the boundless world about him, as measured by the intelligence capable of grasping the whole of truth and knowledge.

Yes, Virginia, there is a Santa Claus. He exists as certainly as love and generosity and devotion exist, and you know that they abound and give to your life its highest beauty and joy. Alas! How dreary would be the world if there were no Santa Claus. It would be as dreary as if there were no Virginias.

There would be no childlike faith then, no poetry, no romance to make tolerable this existence. We should have no enjoyment except in sense and sight. The eternal light with which childhood fills the world would be extinguished.

Not to believe in Santa Claus! You might as well not believe in fairies! You might get your papa to hire men to watch in all the Chimneys on Christmas Eve to catch Santa Claus, but even if they did not see Santa Claus coming down, what would that prove?

Nobody sees Santa Claus, but that is no sign that there is no Santa Claus. The most real things in the world are those that neither children nor men can see. Did you ever see fairies dancing on the lawn? Of course not, but that's no proof that they are not there. Nobody can conceive or imagine all the wonders there are unseen and unseeable in the world.

You tear apart a baby's rattle and see what makes the noise inside, but there is a veil covering the unseen world which not the strongest men, not even the united strength of all the strongest men that ever lived, could tear apart.

Only faith, fancy, poetry, love, romance, can push aside the curtain and view and picture the supernatural beauty and glory beyond. Is it all real? Ah, Virginia, in all this world there is nothing else real and abiding.

No Santa Claus! Thank God he lives, and he lives forever. A thousand years from now, Virginia, nay, ten times ten thousand years from now, he will continue to make glad the heart of childhood.

Either as Saint Nicholas or Santa Claus, the patron of children has consistently been the most popular of all the saints in the heavenly choirs, excluding only Mary, the Mother of God. A few years ago a German scholar, Karl Meisen, counted 2,137 monuments to Saint Nicholas erected before 1500 in France, Germany, Belgium, Luxemburg and the Netherlands.

The monuments we create to honor Nicholas in the United States are neither so monumental nor enduring as those erected in Europe before 1500. We honor Saint Nicholas/Santa Claus by placing his image on millions and millions of Christmas cards and stamps each year and by countless plays presented by children in schools at Christmas time. North Pole, a village in up-state New York, is a theme park about Santa Claus.

Other American monuments that recur each year are Christmas carols that are either addressed to Saint Nicholas or recall the adventures of Santa Claus. In honor of Saint Nicholas/Santa Claus, tunesmiths have created one play, *Miracle on Thirty-Fourth Street* and two scenes in at least two other plays, *Mame*, and *Promises, Promises*. The ancient Bishop of Myra has found a most congenial home in the hearts of the American people, be they seven or seventy years old.

Although for at least the first seven centuries following his death Nicholas was most popular as the patron saint of seafarers, in the past seven centuries he has been acclaimed as the patron saint of children, at least in the Churches outside the realm of Orthodoxy. His patronage embraced almost everything associated with childhood. Thus, for example, Adriaan de Groot, a psychology professor at the University of Amsterdam wrote: "In the Middle Ages, St. Nicholas was not only the protector of children but also the patron of parenthood, the fosterer of family fertility. He must have been invoked many, many times by married couples who wanted children."

For many centuries young maidens in France made pilgrimages to churches dedicated to

Saint Nicholas, seeking his intercession in finding a good husband. In some of the legends, as Martin Ebon observed, "we find Saint Nicholas quite clearly as the Guardian of Children, a patron more profound and humanly valuable, one might say, than a mere Giver of Gifts." One wonders why those so active in the pro-life movement have not turned to Saint Nicholas as their heavenly advocate.

One would hardly imagine, that so noble and generous a saint and symbol would ever be attacked by anyone. But this too has happened to the Gift-giver Saint Nicholas/Jolly Old St. Nick. One example of many attacks on the Holy Gift-Giver occurred in 1981 when an Episcopal priest let fly a broadside against Nicholas. He preached that Nicholas was prowling about at night frightening the daylights out of innocent little children by invading their bedrooms. The preacher waxed eloquently (and aimlessly):

"Though he appears to be a great giver, he is actually a thief. For he is stealing the true value of Christmas. He directs our attention to selfish glitter, money, and a spirit that comes out of a bottle. His bottomless sack feeds our basic emotion and he represents getting rather than giving."

What he said may be true in this age of commercialism.

It definitely has not been accepted, however, by millions and millions "of good little boys and girls," regardless of their age. It would appear that the Episcopal priest never read Church's editorial which hails the virtues Santa Claus portrays.

Nor, it would seem, did he know the works of Dr. Joost A. M. Meerloo, a psychoanalyst who practiced in New York City and wrote:

"In the deepest sense, he [Nicholas] bestows the gift of continual revival upon man, the blessing of children, which were the first reassurances and life investments of his ancestors. He directs the eternal battle between good and evil, and somehow during the long nights of the winter solstice, he gets into everybody's blood to arouse holy and worldly sentiments."

AFTERWORD

October 20, 1994

My Dear Nicholas,

TEN MONTHS HAVE PASSED SINCE I WROTE YOU MY FIRST letter. I have spent most of those months except when I was flat on my back with an infirmity – reading about Saint Nicholas and Santa Claus. I set my hand at writing these pages only during the past three months.

I have gathered together a great deal of information about Saint Nicholas/Santa Claus from the surfeit of books and articles I read. I did, however, so much want to pass on to you what I learned.

During this period of rather extensive reading I came across a passage in the biography of Martin Ebon that seemed, at least to me, the reason for my understanding this work. I suspect it is the same reason why your grandparents make such a fuss over you and your cousins at Christmas-time. He wrote:

"This extreme manifestation of the desire to get something for nothing (or at least in exchange for the right words, the correct ritual) expresses a timeless, universal human hope. The gambler, the race-track habitué, and the buyer of lottery tickets act on similar hopes, beliefs, or delusions. But while the followers of the Cargo Cult are sure to be disappointed… the small child's belief in Santa Claus will be rewarded. This earnest belief, this untainted faith, is based on an innocence that has not yet been wounded by the sharp edges of reality. It is proper, I think, that such innocence be respected. What, indeed, do we have to offer as a replacement for faith and trust? Only knowledge, with all its imperfections. If the spirit of Saint Nicholas lives in our times, it is not to be found during a pilgrimage to the sunken church in Myra (Demre), but among adults who are privileged to see a bright-eyed child discover a gift that Santa Claus had brought during the night."

So much for the explanation of this work. I do wish, however, to leave you a challenge. You will, hopefully, be able to read these pages long after I have, hopefully, joined Saint Nicholas in our heavenly home. We will be awaiting your arrival with a twinkle in our eyes.

I leave you these words, written by Robin Crichton, to ponder when you stand at the threshold of manhood:

"Santa Claus is faced with an identity crisis. He is schizophrenic. Which of all his multiple personalities will triumph in the Christmases to come? Generation after generation families have introduced their children to the legends, and in one guise or another, Santa has survived for over 1700 years. Now he has reached perhaps the biggest crisis of his career and, as in his past, so his future will be a reflection of the values of the society which we in our turn create for the generations to come."

Your loving great-uncle,

Vincent A. Yzermans

Monsignor Vincent A. Yzermans, a priest of the Diocese of St. Cloud, Minnesota, wrote this book, and Brother Placid Stuckenschneider, O.S.B., of St. John's Abbey in Collegeville, Minnesota, designed the interior. It was completed on the Feast of St. Nicholas in the year of Our Lord nineteen hundred and ninety-four. Only 500 copies of the hardcover edition were printed and distributed as a Christmas gift by Park Press Quality Printing, Inc., of Waite Park, Minnesota.

ACTA Publications of Chicago, Illinois, discovered a copy of the book in 2004 and offered to publish it in paperback, with royalties going to the estate of Msgr. Yzermans.

This softcover edition is printed on 80-lb. Finch Vanilla opaque paper. The text is set in 11-point Garamond with Irish uncial capitals. Typesetting by Robert Briggs, with digitizing and processing of artwork and photographs by the staff of Park Press Quality Printing. The new cover is designed by Tom A. Wright.